FROM AN IDEA TO
GOOGLE

FROM AN IDEA TO

GOOGLE

How Innovation at Google Changed the World

LOWEY BUNDY SICHOL

illustrated by C. S. JENNINGS

HOUGHTON MIFFLIN HARCOURT
Boston   New York

hmhbooks.com

The text was set in ITC Galliard Std.

Library of Congress Cataloging-in-Publication Data
Names: Sichol, Lowey Bundy, author.
Title: From an idea to Google / by Lowey Bundy Sichol.
Description: Boston : Houghton Mifflin Harcourt, [2019] | Series:
From an idea to . . . ; 4
Identifiers: LCCN 2018016633 | ISBN 9781328954916
(paper over board) | ISBN 9781328954923 (pbk.)
Subjects: LCSH: Google (Firm)—Juvenile literature. | Google—
Juvenile literature. | Internet industry—
United States—Juvenile literature.
Classification: LCC HD9696.8.U64 G6666 2019 |
DDC 338.7/61025040973—dc23
LC record available at https://lccn.loc.gov/2018016633

Printed in the United States of America
DOC 10 9 8 7 6 5 4 3 2 1
4500759251

For everyone at the Tuck School of Business
at Dartmouth (past, present, and future).

A special thanks to Professor Kevin Lane Keller,
who taught me at Tuck, employed me as a case writer,
and has always provided unparalleled
advice and guidance.

Table of Contents

"We see being great at something as a starting point, not an endpoint."
—Larry Page and Sergey Brin

Have you ever wondered what the *business* story behind Google is?

You probably use Google every day in one way or another. You undoubtedly look for information with Google Search. Maybe you also have a Gmail email account. You might post your schoolwork on Google Docs. And your parents probably get directions and check traffic through Google Maps.

Today, Google is the most popular website in the world. There are close to four million Google searches every minute, which comes out to over two trillion Google searches each year! And Google is much more than a search engine—it owns more than a hundred different products that help make billions of people's lives better and easier.

But before Google changed our lives, it was just an idea. An idea that two friends, Larry Page and Sergey Brin, had while they were studying computer science at Stanford University. This is the story of Google and how it grew from an *idea* to the most valuable company in the world.

1 Larry Page

LARRY'S CHILDHOOD

Larry Page was born on March 26, 1973, in East Lansing, Michigan, the hometown to Michigan State University. Larry's parents were dedicated and devoted to both Larry and his older brother, Carl Jr. They encouraged creativity and intellectual conversation,

"When I was younger and first started thinking about my future, I decided to either become a professor or start a company." —Larry Page

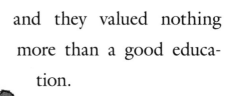

and they valued nothing more than a good education.

Larry's father, Dr. Carl Page, was the first person in his family to graduate high school and attend college. A gifted mathematician, Carl studied engineering and was a pioneer in the field of computer science, earning one of the first computer science PhDs from the University of Michigan. Carl went on to teach computer science at Michigan State University. Larry's mother, Gloria Page, was passionate about computer science as well. She taught computer programming at Lyman Briggs College, a residential college at Michigan State University.

3

As a child, Larry had the same distinctive characteristics he does today—short, straight black hair, thick, dark eyebrows, and a big, toothy smile. Larry attended the Okemos Montessori School in Okemos, Michigan, where he had the freedom to self-direct his education and explore school subjects independently. The environment was perfect for quirky, quiet, and curious Larry.

Back at home, Larry was immersed in a world of computers. He explained, "I was really lucky that my father was a computer science professor, which was unusual for someone my age." One day in 1978, Carl Page purchased and brought home the family's first computer, an Exidy Sorcerer. Larry remembers, "It was huge, and it cost a lot of money, and we couldn't afford to eat well after that." As a young boy, Larry began experimenting with the Exidy Sorcerer. Larry's brother, Carl Jr., recalled, "One of the early things I remember Larry doing was typing *Frog and Toad Together* into his computer, one word at a time."

As Larry got older, he became even more interested in computers. He started doing his homework on the family's latest computer and

printing it out. His teachers were both amazed and confused—no child had ever done that before. When Carl Jr. came home from the University of Michigan with college-level computer homework, he let nine-year-old Larry help him try to solve it. Larry and Carl Jr. were a curious duo, often finding items in their house and taking them apart just to figure out how they worked. One day, Larry and Carl took apart all the family's power tools.

In addition to occasionally deconstructing power tools, Larry read books, as well as the computer, science, and technology magazines left around by his parents. When Larry was twelve years old, he read a book that brought him to tears, and would go on to make a big impact in his future. The book was about

the brilliant inventor and engineer Nikola Tesla. Tesla was best known for inventing the alternating-current electrical system that's used today. However, Tesla never figured out how to create a sustainable business around his inventions and died with little money, fame, or success. Moved by Tesla's tragic ending, Larry began to under-stand how **innovation** alone is not enough.

> **Innovation:** A revolution-ary new way of doing something. This could be a new idea, a new method, or a new product.

The key to success was to *combine* innovative technologies with a successful business strategy.

Larry attended East Lansing's MacDonald Middle School and then East Lansing High School. When he wasn't working hard at school or tinkering with computers, Larry enjoyed music. He played the saxophone and spent two summers at Interlochen Center for the Arts studying music composition. Over time, Larry developed a passion for time, rhythm, and speed in music, which eventually carried over to the way he thought about computing.

After graduating high school in 1991, Larry attended the University of Michigan.

Larry received excellent grades and earned several academic honor awards. He was president of the University of Michigan chapter of Eta Kappa Nu, a national honor society for computer engineering students. Larry was also a member of the University of Michigan's solar car team, the Maize and Blue, and became interested in the future of transportation. At one point, Larry shared his vision for a monorail system that would run between buildings and campuses at the university. Although the monorail was never built, Larry did become a minor celebrity on campus after he built a working ink-jet printer entirely out of LEGO bricks. By the time Larry graduated from the University of Michigan, his only work experience was helping out with the donut stand to raise money for Eta Kappa Nu.

Sergey Brin

SERGEY'S CHILDHOOD

Sergey Brin was born on August 21, 1973, in Moscow, Russia. Sergey was born during a time when Russia was part of a group of countries called the Soviet Union, led by a **communist** government. The Soviet Union

"They see enormous mountains, where I only saw one little hill to climb." —Sergey Brin

> **Communism:** A type of government and economic system in which the government (not individual people) owns and controls everything, including land and factories. Everyone is required to share the wealth that they create in an attempt to establish an equal way of life among everyone. However, communist governments have led to many problems, especially because people are not rewarded for exceptional work.

prevented Jewish people, like Sergey's parents, from studying certain subjects at school or holding certain jobs.

Sergey's father, Mikhail Brin, had always dreamed of being an astronomer, but the Soviet Union forbade him from studying physics, a key subject in astronomy. Instead, Mikhail studied mathematics and attended Moscow State University, which had a very prestigious program. After graduating, Mikhail was again forbidden by the Soviet Union to pursue his goals, which this time was working at the space program. Mikhail settled for a job with the Russian economic policy planning agency, a job he despised. Sergey's mother, Yevgenia Brin, also studied mathematics at Moscow State University, and she took a job in a research laboratory at the Soviet gas and oil institute. Despite Mikhail and Yevgenia's high education and respectable jobs, they felt trapped and could only afford to live in a very small apartment that they shared with Sergey's grandmother, Maya.

In 1977, Mikhail attended an international mathematics conference in Poland. It was there that he met researchers and mathematicians from around the world and realized there were endless opportunities outside of the Soviet Union. When Mikhail returned home, he announced that the Brin family was going to emigrate. He wanted Sergey, Yevgenia, Maya, and himself to be free to pursue their dreams and experience a better life.

In 1979, the Brin family left most of their possessions behind and moved halfway around the world to the United States. Sergey was

FUN FACTS

Sergey took gymnastics as a child and once thought he might run away with the circus.

six years old and only spoke Russian when the family settled in a blue-collar neighborhood in Maryland, near Washington, D.C. Sergey explained, "We started with nothing. We were poor . . . When we first moved to the States we rented a little house, and my parents didn't have a proper room to sleep in. They had to wall off the kitchen. It was a very humble beginning." Despite the hard times, Mikhail and Yevgenia kept their sense of humor, often laughing and joking around with each other, a characteristic that would soon rub off on Sergey.

Mikhail, who changed his name to Michael when he arrived in the United States, and Yevgenia, who changed her name to Eugenia, started to look for work. Fortunately, Russian mathematicians were highly regarded and sought after in the United States. Michael took

a job teaching mathematics at the University of Maryland. Eugenia became a scientist at NASA's Goddard Space Flight Center. One of the projects she worked on was studying how weather conditions affect space travel.

Sergey also settled into a routine. He attended Paint Branch Montessori School in Adelphi, Maryland. At school, Sergey was creative, confident, and fascinated by numbers.

Montessori school allowed Sergey to learn at his own pace, which for Sergey was quite fast. In fact, sometimes Sergey became bored at school, especially in math. It was all too simple for him. To help keep Sergey engaged, Michael and Eugenia began teaching him advanced mathematics and computer programming at home after school. For his ninth birthday, Sergey received a very rare gift from his parents—a personal computer called the Commodore 64.

By the time Sergey entered middle school, he could solve graduate-level math problems and had been labeled by educators as a math genius. Sergey attended Eleanor Roosevelt High School in Greenbelt, Maryland, where he often tried to prove his teachers wrong in front of the other students.

Sergey graduated a year early from high school and was accepted into the University of Maryland. Then, while most students take four years to finish college, Sergey graduated in just three years, with high honors in mathematics and honors in computer science. Sergey's impressive marks earned him a National Science Foundation graduate fellowship, which allowed him to continue his education at Stanford University.

When Sergey arrived at Stanford's prestigious graduate program, he had already mastered many of the courses needed to graduate, so he started to enjoy life a bit more. He was an athletic young man with a slender build, bushy brown hair, big brown eyes, and a contagious laugh. Sergey took up sailing, practiced gymnastics, and mastered the trapeze. He basked in the California sunshine,

socialized with other students, and explored new classes like molecular biology. He also became a tour guide, showing prospective computer science graduate students around the campus. One day, Michael Brin asked Sergey if he was taking any advanced courses and Sergey responded, "Yes, advanced swimming."

LOVE—NOT AT FIRST SIGHT

Although Larry and Sergey were born in different parts of the world and experienced very different childhoods, they still had a lot in common when they first met. Both Larry and Sergey came from highly intellectual Jewish families. Their fathers were both esteemed professors. Each of their mothers had jobs working with computers and technology. They were educated as young children at Montessori schools. Exposure to computers happened early in both of their lives. They excelled in high school and college. And most important, both Larry and Sergey were passionate about mathematics and computer science. It seemed as if they should become instant friends—but that wasn't what happened. In fact, when Larry and Sergey first met, they didn't like each other at all.

The year was 1995. Larry had been admitted to Stanford University to study advanced computer science and was assigned to a tour group. Sergey was his guide.

During that tour of Stanford University, Larry and Sergey spent most of the time arguing with each other. Although few know exactly what they argued about, years later Larry explained how he felt that day: "I thought [Sergey] was pretty obnoxious. He had really strong opinions about things, and I guess I did, too."

3 Searching for an Idea

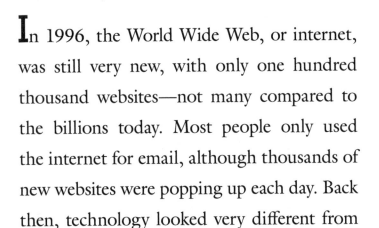

In 1996, the World Wide Web, or internet, was still very new, with only one hundred thousand websites—not many compared to the billions today. Most people only used the internet for email, although thousands of new websites were popping up each day. Back then, technology looked very different from

"Anything you can imagine probably is doable, you just have to imagine it and work on it." —Larry Page

how it looks today. Desktop computers came in two pieces—a monitor and a separate, larger component that included the hard drive and a floppy disk drive. Internet access ran through a cord, with no Wi-Fi. Cell phones had long antennas. Twitter, Instagram, and Facebook didn't exist, and Apple's iPhone wouldn't be invented for another twelve years.

That same year, Larry Page was busy

thinking about his doctoral thesis at Stanford University. A doctoral thesis is a project where graduate students try to figure out a solution to a complicated problem and write a long report about it.

Larry had an idea for his doctoral thesis. He was intrigued by the internet and how **search engines** retrieved websites. Back then,

> **Search engine:** A program that searches for and identifies items in a database that correspond to keywords specified by the user. Search engines are used to find particular websites or information on the internet.

search engines like Yahoo, AltaVista, HotBot, and Excite existed, but they searched for results by scanning every single website looking for keywords. That meant the websites with the highest number of keywords—the words a user typed into the search engine—showed up first.

Larry didn't think using keywords produced good results for two reasons. One, with so many new websites launching each day, it took a *very long time* for early search engines to scan all the websites and bring up results. Two, early search engines did not have a system in place to consider how *important* the information on each website was. This meant that looking for websites with the highest number of keywords on them often retrieved irrelevant and illogical results.

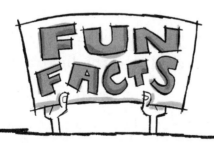

In 1989, an English engineer and computer scientist named Tim Berners-Lee invented the World Wide Web.

AN IDEA TO RANK DIFFERENTLY

Larry had an idea. Instead of ranking websites based on the number of keywords, Larry wanted to rank websites by how many *other* websites linked to them. It was comparable to how citations work. Citations are the way academic research papers reference back to other papers. "Citations are important," Larry explained. "It turns out, people who win the Nobel Prize have citations from ten thousand different papers."

Larry took his ranking idea one step further. He believed that the links coming from other websites differed in importance, too. He considered the links coming from popular websites (those also with lots of links to them) to be more important than the links coming from less popular websites (those with few links to them).

Larry started working on a link-ranking system and called it PageRank, appropriately named after his last name.

FORMING A SEARCH PARTY

By now, Sergey and Larry had put their initial disagreements behind them and had become good friends. Larry knew that Sergey was a mathematical genius and believed that his exceptional skills would be critical to calculating the mathematical structure between all the internet's links. Sergey was intrigued by the idea of analyzing huge amounts of data for Larry's PageRank project. They decided to partner up and soon realized they were a great team.

BACKRUB, THEIR FIRST SEARCH ENGINE

Larry and Sergey got to work. They downloaded the entire World Wide Web onto their computers and started analyzing its links and ranking websites. They worked for many hours every single day, even on weekends and holidays. Larry remembers, "We started working really, really hard on it. There was an important lesson for us."

By early 1997, Larry and Sergey had developed their first search engine, called BackRub, to test out how well PageRank

Google was first written with an exclamation point—Google! This is most likely because Yahoo!, the number one search engine at the time, also had an exclamation point.

worked. The initial results were astounding. BackRub produced useful search results in a logical order of importance, and in a fraction of the time of other search engines. Sergey explained, "We saw that a thousand results weren't necessarily as useful as ten good ones."

AN ACCIDENTAL NAME

By the fall of 1997, BackRub was a superior search engine. But Larry and Sergey wanted to come up with a new name that was catchy and more interesting. For days, they wrote different names on a whiteboard and rejected them.

One day, a classmate named Sean Anderson suggested "Googolplex." It was a mathematical term—the numeral one followed by a googol zeros. Larry liked it but wanted something shorter and asked, "How about we try Googol?"

In 1929, mathematician Edward Kasner asked his nine-year-old nephew, Milton Sirotta, to help him come up with a name for the mathematical number one followed by one hundred zeros. As the two walked through the New Jersey Palisades, Milton suggested the name "googol." He then suggested there should be a bigger number called "googolplex," which would be one followed by "writing zeros until you get tired." Today, "googolplex" is defined as one followed by a googol zeros.

That was also a mathematical term—the numeral one followed by one hundred zeros. Sean accidentally misspelled "Googol" and typed "Google" into the internet to see if the website name was available. Google.com was available and they registered it immediately. However, the next morning Larry and Sergey realized Sean's spelling mistake. A quick look online revealed that the correctly spelled domain name, www.googol.com, was *not* available, so Google was officially born . . . by accident.

ENGINEERING THE GOOGLE LOGO

Logo: A picture or symbol that companies use to identify themselves. Logos come in all shapes, sizes, and colors.

With a new name came a new **logo**. Larry and Sergey wanted the Google logo to be simple, with a clean font and bright colors. The result was a multicolored, almost childlike "Google," where G = blue, o = red, o = yellow, g = blue, l = green, and e = red. The word was placed upon a white background.

FUN FACTS

Other people often misspell the name Google, too, so the company also owns the domain names www.gogle.com and www.googlr.com, which point to the correct www.google.com.

4 In Search of the Future

Larry and Sergey quickly learned that running Google was time-consuming and required lots of expensive computer equipment. Since they had little money, they bought parts and built their own computers. Sometimes they "borrowed" unclaimed equipment from Stanford's loading dock. Sergey explained,

"You should try to do things most people would not."—Larry Page

"We would just borrow a few machines, figuring if they didn't pick it up right away, they didn't need it so badly." Soon, both of their dorm rooms had turned into overflowing data centers.

To stay organized, Larry built storage containers out of LEGO bricks. They turned out to be perfect for the job—inexpensive, durable, and easy to change into various sizes.

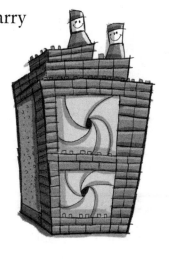

GOOGLE FOR SALE

Before long, most of the students at Stanford University were using Google. It was powerful, smart, fast, and easy to use—much better than any search engine before it. But as Google grew in popularity, a new problem arose. Larry and Sergey were having a hard time juggling Google and being full-time students. Running Google took up all their time.

Larry and Sergey discussed their options. They could sell Google and stay in school. Or, they could leave Stanford and focus all their effort on launching Google as a real company. Both men were torn. Larry's father, Carl, had recently died from complications lingering from having polio as a child. He knew how much his Stanford education meant to his dad,

FUN FACTS

Today, people wonder if the colors in the Google logo—which look very similar to the colors of LEGO bricks—were inspired by the LEGO shelves in their dorm room.

and thought staying in school might be a nice tribute. Sergey was torn because he wasn't sure that all the hard work of running a company was for him. They decided to try to sell Google.

Larry and Sergey approached AltaVista in the hopes of selling Google for one million dollars. When AltaVista turned them down, Larry and Sergey approached other search engines, including Yahoo! and Excite, but they said no as well. In fact, every single company Larry and Sergey approached did not want to buy Google.

TAKING A RISK

After being rejected so many times, Sergey turned to a trusted professor and asked for advice on whether he should stay in school or leave Stanford to focus on Google. The professor turned to Sergey and said, "Look, if this Google thing pans out, then great. If not, you can return to graduate school and finish your thesis."

It was decided. Larry and Sergey packed up their belongings and left Stanford University, hoping to turn Google into a successful company.

5

Launching to the World

Larry and Sergey needed two things before they could launch Google—a place to work and money to help run the business. In August 1998, the two men reached out to a man named Andy Bechtolsheim, who was the cofounder of a company called Sun Microsystems. Andy liked the idea of

"It's often easier to make progress when you're really ambitious. Since no one else is willing to try those things you don't have any competition." —Larry Page

Google, proclaiming, "This is the single best idea I have heard in years. I want to be part of this." He handed Larry and Sergey a check for $100,000, making him the first person to **invest** in Google. In exchange for the money, Andy received a portion of the profits as Google grew bigger. (It was a good investment. Fifteen years later, Andy's $100,000 was worth $1,700,000,000!)

Invest: Giving money to a company or enterprise with the expectation that it will become successful and profitable, making money for the investor.

Google now needed an office space. A friend of Sergey's named Susan Wojcicki offered to rent them her garage for $1,700 a month. Larry and Sergey accepted the offer, packed up their computers and equipment, and set up Google's first headquarters in Susan's garage in Menlo Park, California. On September 4, 1998, Google launched to the world.

FUN FACTS

Susan Wojcicki, the woman whose garage became the first Google headquarters, was the sixteenth employee hired at Google. In 2014, she became the CEO of YouTube, which Google owns.

RAISING MONEY

Almost immediately, stories about Google's search engine appeared in newspapers and magazines across the country. Most reporters gushed over the speed and accuracy of Google's search engine, claiming that this start-up company from Stanford University was changing the way the internet worked. Just two months after launching, *PC Magazine* named Google a search engine of choice.

It became clear that to keep up with demand, Larry and Sergey needed even more money so they could hire additional engineers and purchase sufficient computer equipment. Between friends and family, they quickly raised one million dollars.

Google's first employee was a fellow PhD student from

Stanford named Craig Silverstein. Within five months, Google had eight employees—all engineers—and had outgrown Susan's garage. They moved into an office on University Avenue in Palo Alto, California.

By early 1999, Google was handling over a hundred thousand search queries a day and growing fast. In fact, demand for Google was so high that money became an issue again. They needed significantly more money to help purchase the equipment and hire the employees necessary to keep up with such a fast pace of growth.

Larry and Sergey turned to two **venture capital firms**, Kleiner Perkins and Sequoia

Venture capital firm: A company that provides a financial investment to start-up companies and small businesses in hopes that they will have long-term growth.

Capital. Both firms were impressed with Larry and Sergey and their vision for Google. Kleiner Perkins and Sequoia Capital each agreed to invest $12.5 million in Google under one condition: Larry and Sergey had to hire an experienced person to become the CEO of Google. This new CEO would help figure out how Google would make money. Larry and Sergey agreed to the condition and soon had $25 million in the bank. Good thing, too, because Google had outgrown its office space again. Google soon moved into a larger office space at 2400 Bayshore Parkway in Mountain View, California.

6

Let's Be the Good Guys

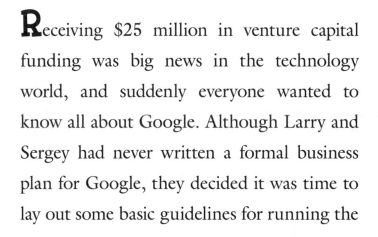

Receiving $25 million in venture capital funding was big news in the technology world, and suddenly everyone wanted to know all about Google. Although Larry and Sergey had never written a formal business plan for Google, they decided it was time to lay out some basic guidelines for running the

"If you're not doing some things that are crazy, then you're doing the wrong things." —Larry Page

company. Larry and Sergey wrote Google's mission: "To organize the world's information and make it universally accessible and useful." They also wrote "Ten things we know to be true," which was a guideline for running their business. Included in the "Ten things" was a version of Google's founding credo, or motto: "Don't be evil." It meant that Google would always be one of the "good guys" in business, striving to do the right thing for the good of the world, especially in the long term.

GOOGLE'S 10 THINGS

1. Focus on the user and all else will follow.
2. It's best to do one thing really, really well.
3. Fast is better than slow.
4. Democracy on the web works.
5. You don't need to be at your desk to need an answer.
6. You can make money without doing evil.
7. There's always more information out there.
8. The need for information crosses all borders.
9. You can be serious without a suit.
10. Great just isn't good enough.

GOOGLE DOODLES

In August 1999, Larry and Sergey decided to take a break from the stresses of Google and attend a festival in the middle of the Nevada desert called Burning Man. It was a multi-day event celebrating artists from around the world. Larry and Sergey wanted their users to know that they were away from the office in case anything happened to the website, so they placed the logo of the Burning Man festival (a

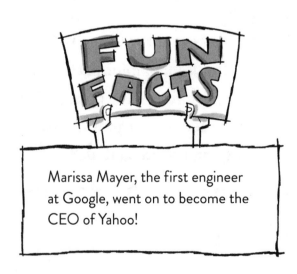

Marissa Mayer, the first engineer at Google, went on to become the CEO of Yahoo!

stick figure) behind the second
o in the Google logo.

A few months later, near
the end of October, Sergey called one of
Google's top engineers into his office, a woman
named Marissa Mayer. Sergey said to her, "We
should show people in the world that people at
Google care about Halloween." He asked that
she post a Halloween-themed version of the
Google logo he had designed, complete with
pumpkins as *o*'s in the Google logo.

Turned out, users liked the funny logo and
wanted more. Sergey liked them, too, and suggested, "What about aliens? Let's put aliens
on the homepage. We'll change it every day.
It will be like a comic strip that people come
back to read."

Sergey and his team named the different

versions of Google's logo "Doodles." Soon there were Doodles for Valentine's Day, Easter, and yes, even alien Doodles. Over the years, the responsibility of creating Doodles has shifted to an entire team of designers, engineers, and graphic artists. They now appear on holidays, anniversaries, and days that celebrate a leader, artist, pioneer, or scientist.

Every day, Google Trends reports what the most searched topics are in different categories. In 2016, "Chicago Cubs" was the number one searched sports team in the world, "Happy Birthday to You" was the number one searched song in the world, and "green bean casserole" was the number one searched recipe in the world.

APRIL FOOLS!

Sergey, much like his parents, was known for his witty sense of humor. In addition to designing Doodles and playing practical jokes on others, he loved April Fool's Day. On April 1, 2000, Sergey and some other Googlers decided to launch an April Fool's joke on Google users. They released an announcement on their homepage that Google had a new mind-reading technology called MentalPlex.

Google claimed that by removing one's hat and glasses and staring into a swirly red-and-blue ball on the homepage, and then clicking on it, users would have their minds read by MentalPlex. This, of course, was not possible, so once the user clicked on the ball, "April Fools!" popped up on the screen.

Since then, Google has unveiled many more April Fool's Day jokes, mostly announcing fake products that allowed users to do crazy things. There was Google gBall, which could determine how hard rugby players threw and kicked the ball; Google Motion, which allowed users to spell out search words by forming letters with their bodies; and Google Nose, which allowed users to smell what they searched for.

7 In Search of Googleyness

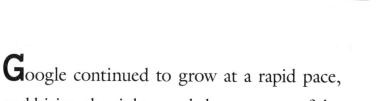

Google continued to grow at a rapid pace, and hiring the right people became one of the most important things Larry and Sergey did. The two men insisted their employees—or "Googlers"—have excellent grades, high SAT scores, and a certain sense of "Googleyness." That meant every Googler must work well

"We do go out of our way to recruit people who are a little different."
—Larry Page

with others and contribute something unique to Google.

Larry and Sergey traveled all over the world—from the Middle East to Europe to Russia—seeking out the most talented engineers. Sometimes, Larry and Sergey came up with clever ways to identify the brightest engineers in the world. They even had a billboard constructed that read:

"{first 10-digit prime found in consecutive digits of *e*}.com"

The answer to the billboard's riddle was 7427466391. When a person typed www.742

7466391.com into their internet browser, it led to another riddle, which ultimately led to a page on Google's recruiting website that stated, "One thing we learned while building Google is that it's easier to find what you're looking for if it comes looking for you. What we're looking for are the best engineers in the world. And here you are."

Engineers played such an important role in the future of Google that Larry and Sergey personally interviewed every single engineer, often asking challenging questions. Sergey liked to ask candidates, "Could you teach me something complicated I don't know?"

Google hired its first head chef, Charlie Ayers, in 1999. One day he served lobsters that were on sale because they only had one claw.

Larry, who was soft-spoken and much more reserved than Sergey, would often ask himself whether a candidate could pass his airport test. "Just think about if you got stuck in an airport with this [job candidate], on a long layover on a business trip," Larry explained. "Would you be happy or sad about it?" Needless to say, interviews with Larry and Sergey were not boring. Once, on Halloween, Sergey conducted an interview while dressed in a full-size cow costume. Another time, Sergey conducted an interview while wearing Rollerblades and athletic shorts.

New employees were called Nooglers. One day, a Noogler named Jim Reese showed up at Google for his first day of work. He had gone to Harvard,

Yale Medical School, and studied to be a neurosurgeon at Stanford. On his first day of work, Larry said, "Here's your space over here. There are a bunch of parts over there. Make your own computer."

INSPIRING INNOVATION

To help foster innovation and encourage creativity among its engineers, Larry and Sergey

Your own Google Doodle design could be on Google's homepage. Every year, Google runs a Doodle 4 Google contest for kids. More than one million doodles are submitted by students. The winning doodle is featured on google.com, and the creator receives a trip to Google's headquarters. Good luck!

established some rules early on. Borrowed from the academic world, Larry and Sergey instituted the 20 percent rule. That meant all engineers could take 20 percent of their week—or one full day—to work on anything they wanted to. This level of freedom encouraged engineers to think creatively about things they were passionate about—robots, astronomy, animals, maps, books—and dream of the unimaginable. Some of Google's greatest products evolved from the 20 percent rule, including Gmail, Google Now, Google News, Google Sky, and Street View on Google Maps.

Larry and Sergey also created an environment where Googlers naturally shared their ideas with each other. Engineers were required to post all their projects in a database where the other engineers could view, comment, critique, or expand

on these ideas. Googlers sat in open cubicles instead of offices with doors. Even Larry and Sergey shared an office. Googlers attended a weekly meeting called TGIF where Nooglers wore Google multicolored beanie hats topped with a propeller so other Googlers could identify them, and anyone could ask Larry and Sergey questions about anything.

FUN FACTS

At Google, Sergey sometimes walks around on his hands, bounces on a big rubber ball, and swings from the ceiling rafters.

8 Google's Search for Profitability

Google Search soon became the most popular search engine in the world, but Larry and Sergey still had to figure out a way for the company to make money. Like many things on the internet, Google was free to use. People visited www.google.com, typed in their search words, and results appeared.

"Always deliver more than expected." —Larry Page

Many internet companies that were free to use made money by putting flashy advertisements on their websites. But Google's homepage was simple, clean, and free of ads. Larry and Sergey did not want to change any of that. They thought traditional advertisements were distracting and misleading—sometimes even teetering on the edge of "evil."

Then Larry thought about it differently. He wondered, "What if ads weren't intrusive and annoying? What if we could deliver a relevant ad at just the right time and give people useful commercial information?"

ADVERTISING THAT WORKS

In 2000, Google launched an advertising program called AdWords. AdWords made it possible for a company's advertisement to appear *only* when a person searched for something similar to the ad. For example, a search for children's bedroom furniture might reveal an AdWords ad for Pottery Barn Kids, or a search for a Red Sox jersey could reveal an AdWords ad for Dick's Sporting Goods. Ads were clearly marked text boxes that linked to the advertiser's website. No flashy banner

Google Ad Grants gives many nonprofit organizations $10,000 worth of free advertising space each month to help promote their initiatives.

ads or graphics cluttered Google's website or slowed down its search engine. Shortly after AdWords launched, users discovered Google's advertising links were often just as useful as Google's search results and the program took off.

A NEW CEO

With its advertising program now in place, Larry and Sergey needed to make good on their promise to hire a CEO. Over a year had passed since they had raised the $25 million, but Larry and Sergey didn't think anyone was good enough for the job.

Then, one day, a man named Eric Schmidt

entered the picture. Eric was the CEO of a company called Novell and *not* interested in becoming CEO at Google. However, through a mutual friend, Eric agreed to meet with Larry and Sergey. During the meeting, Sergey and Eric became engaged in a heated intellectual discussion about the way Eric was running Novell. "We argued for at least ninety minutes,"

Eric remembered. By the end of the meeting, Eric was intrigued with Sergey and Google, and claimed it was the best  argument he had had in a very long time. Larry and Sergey were equally impressed with Eric's computer science background and experience leading large technology companies. Before long, Eric Schmidt was hired as the CEO of Google.

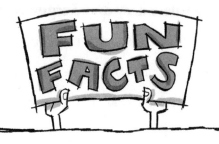

FUN FACTS

Googlers love practical jokes. One day, after Eric Schmidt had been hired as CEO, someone purchased a red telephone booth and had it delivered to Eric's office for no apparent reason other than to be funny.

9 Thinking Outside the Search Box

Larry, Sergey, and Eric made a powerful team. Eric handled the business side of Google, while Larry and Sergey continued to improve Google's search engine and focus on future projects. Before long, the three leaders felt it was time to take the company public.

"Our job is to think of the thing you haven't thought of yet that you really need." —Larry Page

Google **went public** (see page 74) on August 19, 2004, at $85 per share—and raised $1.9 billion.

TWO WAYS TO GROW

As a public company, Larry, Sergey, and Eric wanted to expand Google beyond searches. There are two main ways a company can grow or expand beyond its core business. One is to develop *new* products and services through innovation. The second way is to **acquire,** or

Acquire: To purchase another company. When one company buys another company, it is called an acquisition. After an acquisition, the buying company possesses all the combined assets and technologies, and employs people from both companies. The buying company is also now responsible for every customer.

buy, other companies. Acquisitions can be a good strategy when a company believes it's easier to acquire another company with certain products and technologies rather than to develop them itself.

Over the next decade, Google launched a plethora of new products and services through innovation and acquisition. In fact, between 2001 and 2017, Google spent over $30 billion acquiring more than two hundred companies that specialized in areas such as advertising, navigation, drones, artificial intelligence, and robotics.

Thousands of products are introduced to consumers every year. Some become popular, but not every idea is a good one. New Coke, Purple Ketchup, and Celery Jell-O were all real products that failed.

SOME OF GOOGLE'S MOST POPULAR PRODUCTS

 GMAIL (2004)—A fast, searchable email service with more storage and less spam.

GOOGLE EARTH (2005)—A program that allows users to see the world as never before with satellite images from space. Users can get an in-depth look at different terrains and buildings in 3D, and also see the bottom of the ocean, the moon, and Mars.

 GOOGLE MAPS (2005)—A service that allows users to view maps, satellite images, and directions with real-time traffic.

ANDROID (2005)—A mobile operating system that makes it possible for applications to work on smartphones. Android is an open-source technology, one that is free and available to everyone.

 YOUTUBE (2006)—A video-sharing website where users can upload or view videos for free.

GOOGLE CALENDAR (2006)—A calendar that helps keep track of events, appointments, and birthdays, and can be shared with others, including family and friends.

GOOGLE DOCS (2007)—An online word processor that gives users the ability to open, edit, and create documents, and then share them between students and teachers at school or colleagues in business.

GOOGLE CHROME (2008)—A web browser built for speed, simplicity, and security.

GOOGLE PLAY (2012)—Google's app store for the Android operating system, which allows users to purchase music, movies, and books, and store them in the cloud.

GOOGLE DRIVE (2012)—A cloud-storage service that gives users a way to create, share, and keep all their documents and files in one place.

GOOGLE PHOTOS (2015)—A free photo storage service that automatically organizes users' pictures.

THE GIFT OF FAILURE

Google has always had a positive attitude toward failure. Eric Schmidt explained, "We try things. Remember, we *celebrate* our failures. This is a company where it's absolutely okay to try something that's very hard, have it not be successful, and take the learning from that." Sergey agreed, once stating, "The only way you are going to have success is to have lots of failures first." And there were plenty of failures at Google.

Take, for example, Google Wave. Google Wave was a hyped-up but complicated product that no one seemed to understand. Google Wave launched in 2009 and combined email, text, images, web links, and videos into a communications chain that could involve multiple users. However, Google Wave was very confusing and never took off. Within a few months, it was clear that Google Wave was a flop, and the product was canceled the following year. However, engineers at Google were not punished for launching a failed product. In fact, many were asked to work on other important projects, because Googlers value the risk associated with launching ambitious products.

Google Glass was another famous Google failure. Google Glass was a pair of eyeglasses that cost $1,500 and acted much like a cell phone. The glasses included a camera, a tiny microphone, a speaker by the right ear, and a small screen by the right eye that projected answers to simple commands like "look up current events" or "what is the weather" or "give me directions to the soccer field." Sergey spent a lot of time and energy working on Google

 Glass. However, it soon became clear that users didn't want to pay the expensive price or wear the nerdy-looking glasses when they could easily get more from their cell phones. To Sergey's dismay, Google Glass was discontinued just two years after launching.

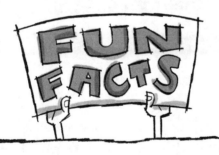

In 2006, Google had become so successful and popular that the word "google" was added to the Merriam-Webster and Oxford English Dictionaries. To "google" is defined as searching for something or someone on the internet using the search engine Google.

WHAT DOES "GOING PUBLIC" MEAN?

Every new company starts off as a **private company** or a **privately held company.** That means the founders who started the business own the entire company and run it the way they want. The founders make all the key decisions for the company. These decisions are private information and not shared with the public.

Some founders may want to switch from being a private company to being a **public company** or a **publicly held company.** When a company goes public, it can raise a lot of money by selling off **"shares of stock,"** or bits of ownership, to anyone who is willing to pay the price. That means the *public* will now own part of the company.

One way to think about going public is to think of a company as a building. Each brick of the building is like a share of stock.

1.5 MILLION BRICKS →

When a company is private, the founders and private investors own all the bricks of the building (or the entire company).

When a company goes public, the founders and private investors sell off a specific number of bricks (or shares of stock) for money—so other people now have a chance to own some of the company. The people who buy and own these shares are called **shareholders**. The price for each brick (or share) can range from a few cents to thousands of dollars based on how well the company is doing. The more each brick (or share) is worth, the more valuable the building (or company) is worth.

WHY DO STOCK PRICES GO UP AND DOWN?

A company can have a high or low stock price for many reasons. A high stock price usually means the company's products are selling well, it is making lots of money, and good leaders are in place. Most people want to own shares of stock in a company that is doing very well and is expected to grow bigger, so the price goes up.

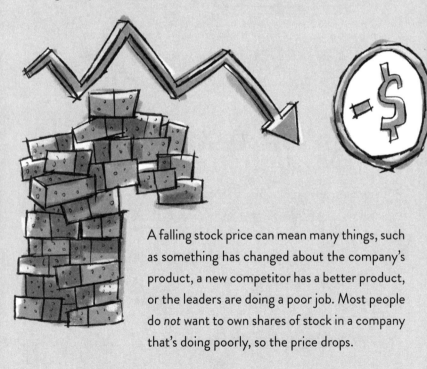

A falling stock price can mean many things, such as something has changed about the company's product, a new competitor has a better product, or the leaders are doing a poor job. Most people do *not* want to own shares of stock in a company that's doing poorly, so the price drops.

The more shares someone holds in one company, the more ownership he or she possesses. For example, while many people own shares of Google, Larry and Sergey have made sure that they own enough shares to maintain control of the company.

WHY DO COMPANIES GO PUBLIC?

The main reason companies decide to go public is to raise money. They can use this money to expand into new areas, develop new products, acquire new companies, hire more people, or pay off debt.

That might sound like a good deal, but there are challenges, too. When a company goes public, there are lots (sometimes tens of millions) of people who now own a little bit of the company. In addition, a public company must follow the rules and regulations set by a department of the U.S. government called the Securities and Exchange Commission (SEC).

The job of the SEC is to protect investors from any sort of dishonest business. The SEC makes and enforces strict rules and regulations that all public companies must follow.

Not every company believes going public is worth the effort of having to follow these rules and regulations or sharing its company information with the public.

10 Googleplex

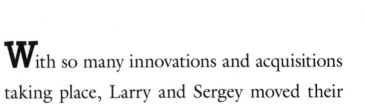

With so many innovations and acquisitions taking place, Larry and Sergey moved their headquarters to a much larger, permanent location in Mountain View, California, appropriately named Googleplex. With over seven million square feet of office space, it's like owning all the office space in the Empire

"We want Google to be the third half of your brain."
—Sergey Brin

EMPIRE STATE BUILDING + WILLIS TOWER = GOOGLEPLEX

State Building in New York City and the Willis Tower (formerly the Sears Tower) in Chicago put together!

Larry and Sergey have designed Googleplex to be a place that harnesses creativity, teamwork, and intellectual growth, and creates opportunities for inspiration. Googleplex is filled with video games, pianos, pools, bowling alleys, climbing walls, a soccer field, pool tables, Ping-Pong tables, foosball, air hockey, beach volleyball courts, and a giant ball pit. Inside, fun and inspirational art hangs on

the walls, including paintings by employees. Outside, a large LEGO man, a life-size model spaceship, oversize shark fins, plastic pink flamingos, and a life-size replica of a dinosaur skeleton named Stan grace the property. Sometimes the plastic pink flamingos end up in Stan's mouth or on his head.

FUN FACTS

In the Googleplex lobby, a live search board displays a scrolling list of search terms people are looking up at that moment, all over the world.

GOOGLEY FOR DOGS

Yoshka, a large furry Leonberger, was the first dog to come to work at Google back in 1999. His job was to lie by the front door and greet the UPS and FedEx delivery people when they arrived with packages. Today, many dogs come to work at Googleplex.

BRAIN FOOD

Larry and Sergey treat their employees very well and have always believed in feeding their employees for free. They recognized early on that keeping Googlers happy, at the office, and

among their fellow colleagues essentially paid for itself. In the beginning, Larry and Sergey provided Googlers with Swedish Fish candy and boxes of cereal that were labeled "Larry-O's" (Cheerios) and "Raisin Brin" (Raisin Bran). Today, dozens of cafés and restaurants throughout Googleplex feed Googlers and their families with healthy, gourmet meals. There is even a café named after Yoshka, the first Google dog.

GOOGLE GOES GREEN

Googleplex is environmentally conscious, too. Built to strict specifications, Google does all it can to create a healthy work space for its people and the planet. One hundred percent of the facility's energy comes from renewable sources such as solar, wind, or water power. Googleplex has solar panels on its rooftop and

MUNCH
MUNCH

FUN FACTS

Google rents goats to clear away long grass and shrubs at their Googleplex headquarters. It takes a week for two hundred goats to trim the grass (by eating it) and fertilize the ground (by pooping it out!). The cost of renting the goats is about the same as mowing the grass with lawn mowers but, as Google reported, "goats are a lot cuter to watch than lawn mowers."

uses wind-harnessed power from wind farms. Kitchens, restaurants, and bathrooms are cleaned with nontoxic products.

Even getting to and around Googleplex is good for the environment. Shuttles transport thousands of employees to work. Once there, Googlers can hop on one of thousands of multicolored bikes called GBikes that look similar to the Google logo, complete with bright yellow-and-red frame, blue handlebars, and green tires. If a bike needs repair, the rider simply places the bike's seat into the basket and the GBikes repair team swings by, picks up the broken bike, and repairs it back at the GBikes repair shop.

11

Behind Door X

Located at the edge of Googleplex, in a three-story red brick building, is one of the most secretive labs in the world—a place called X. X is where Larry, Sergey, and only a couple hundred handpicked employees work on ideas for products and services that one day may solve *huge* problems in the world.

"We should be building great things that don't exist."
—Larry Page

MOONSHOTS

Larry and Sergey call the ideas brewing in X's labs "Moonshots." Moonshots are risky, expensive projects that try to solve impossible  problems. And if a Moonshot project succeeds, it could revolutionize the world, potentially changing the lives of billions of people. Pills that can detect cancer, kites that generate energy from wind, flying cars, and delivery drones are a handful of the Moonshot projects that the public knows about. But most of the secrets behind X's doors remain a secret until Google is ready to share them.

GOOGLE TAKES THE WHEEL

A self-driving car was a Moonshot that has now become a reality, and is making its way onto roads across the country. Google's engineers first explored the idea of self-driving vehicles by removing the steering wheels and pedals and installing software, sensors like lasers and radar, and cameras that detect objects

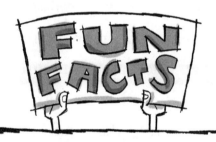

Every year, Google awards scholarships to outstanding women studying computer science in three geographic locations: North America, Africa/Europe/Middle East, and Asia Pacific. The scholarship is called "Women Techmakers" and is given in honor of Dr. Anita Borg, a "technology rebel" who believed in creating equal opportunities for women and minorities in the field of computer science.

all around the car. These sensors can identify objects as far as two hundred yards away (that's two football fields) and in all directions. They can detect pedestrians, cyclists, and even a plastic bag flying in the wind. Special software chooses a safe speed and understands how to avoid cyclists and slow down for pedestrians. Backup software and braking systems make sure that even if one system fails to work, the backup system will replace it and ensure a safe ride. Next, engineers gave the self-driving car a rounded shape. This design helps the sensors see better around the vehicle. Meanwhile, the inside of Google's self-driving car was designed for riders, not drivers. There is plenty of leg room and comfortable seats. Riders might not even notice that there isn't a steering wheel!

Larry and Sergey believe that self-driving cars will transform mobility by making it easier, safer, and more enjoyable to get around. Consider individuals who otherwise wouldn't be able to drive themselves, such as a blind person, someone in a wheelchair, or an elderly person. Consider the fact that there are one million traffic deaths each year, the majority of which are caused by human error. Self-driving cars would eliminate the human-error element, potentially saving thousands of lives every single day.

PROJECT LOON
TAKES FLIGHT

Years ago, Larry, Sergey, and their X employees started working on a Moonshot called Project Loon that is now bringing internet access to remote parts of the world, in areas such as Africa, New Zealand, and South America. Project Loon is a network of helium-filled balloons that beam down internet access. When inflated, the Loon balloons are huge—thirty-nine feet tall and forty-nine feet wide, about the size of a small plane. Each balloon is powered by solar energy and hovers at the edge of space in the stratosphere, which is twice as high as commercial airplanes fly and more than twelve miles above the earth's surface. Once the balloons are there, each one sends internet

access down to an area below it about the size of Rhode Island.

ONLINE WITH LOON

A farmer in New Zealand became the first person to connect to the internet from a Project Loon balloon. Today, thousands of people in remote areas can experience uninterrupted internet access through Loon balloons. But it is not easy to pull off. Google has built a custom-made Autolauncher that looks like a big construction crane, but is specifically designed to gently inflate the Loon balloons and release them into the wind. The Autolauncher inflates and releases one Loon balloon every thirty minutes—that's forty-eight new Loon balloons launched every day. Once launched, Google's "mission control" tracks each balloon and directs it to the areas where it needs to be, keeping in mind how the wind is blowing. After approximately a hundred days, the Loon balloons are safely controlled back down to the earth and collected by Googlers. If for some reason a Loon balloon pops or deflates and starts falling toward the earth, an emergency parachute deploys and carries it safely to the ground.

12 ABCDEF
Google

By 2015, Google had expanded to over 150 different languages and over one billion Gmail accounts, and it was earning over $60 billion in advertising revenue. Larry and Sergey decided it was the right time to restructure their company.

"We won't stop asking 'What if?' and then working hard to find the answer."
—Larry Page and Sergey Brin

WELCOME TO ALPHABET

Larry and Sergey formed a parent company called Alphabet. "Alphabet is mostly a collection of companies," Larry explained. Under the Alphabet umbrella is Google, along with several other companies, including CapitalG, which invests in long-term businesses; GV (formerly Google Ventures), which funds exciting new start-ups; Fiber, which provides internet access; Calico, which works on fighting

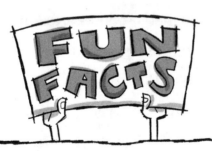

On February 26, 2009, Google sent out its first tweet on Twitter. It read, "I'm 01100110 01100101 01100101 01101100 01101001 01101110 01100111 00100000 01101100 01110101 01100011 01101011 01111001 00001010." This message, which was encoded in binary, means "I'm feeling lucky."

diseases; Nest, which creates smart home products; and X, where secretive Moonshot projects are developed. The new structuring

allowed Google to focus on its core products like Search, Gmail, Maps, Android, and AdWords. On the flip side, Larry and Sergey run Alphabet, which means that their vision to make the world a better place is spread across all of Alphabet's companies. Eric Schmidt stepped down as an executive of Google and Alphabet in 2017 and Larry and Sergey appointed a man named Sundar Pichai to be the CEO of Google. Larry explained, "Our model is to have a strong CEO who runs each business, with Sergey and me in service to them as needed."

FROM AN IDEA TO NOW

Larry and Sergey have come a long way from having an idea and working late nights in their dorm rooms in hopes of making that idea a reality. From their revolutionary search engine to self-driving cars to the secrets bubbling within X's labs, Google has changed the world for billions of people.

But it's not only the innovative products that make Google so successful—it's also the people. Led by two brilliant men with big ideas and strong values, the Google atmosphere is exciting, powerful, and meaningful. And, just as Larry and Sergey explored their idea for a better search engine with a sense of freedom, energy, and willingness to do good, Google engineers are given the freedom to explore their passions and create amazing things every day.

WHAT WILL THE FUTURE OF GOOGLE LOOK LIKE?

Today, Google is not only focused on improving the world with their products, they are also preparing the next generation of engineers, leaders, learners, and explorers. Within schools and classrooms, students and teachers can explore mysterious places like the bottom of the ocean or the surface of Mars with Google Expeditions, a virtual-reality teaching tool. Children can learn about unknown parts of the world such as Uluṟu-Kata Tjuṯa National Park in Australia, and the Anangu ancient traditions and stories. Budding artists can express themselves with a Google 3D drawing tool called Tilt Brush, which allows children to paint in a virtual-reality space with life-size brush strokes. And Google's CS First clubs provide lessons in computer science and fun activities for aspiring engineers. Google has also helped hundreds of thousands of refugee children and parents by providing internet access and educational resources.

Larry and Sergey will be forever known as the two men behind the idea for Google, but their reach today is much further than a search engine. Perhaps their impact on the world is best summed up by what Sergey once said— "Everyone wants to be successful but I want to be looked back on as being very innovative, very trusted and ethical and ultimately making a big difference in the world."

Larry and Sergey have special permission from NASA to take off and land their private airplane on a restricted NASA runway near Googleplex.

Timeline of Google

1973 • Larry Page is born in East Lansing, Michigan. Sergey Brin is born in Moscow, Russia.

1979 • Sergey's family moves from Russia to Maryland.

1995 • Larry and Sergey meet at Stanford University.

1996 • Larry and Sergey create a new website ranking system, called PageRank, and launch their first search engine, called BackRub.

1997 • Larry and Sergey rename their search engine Google, inspired by the mathematical number googol—1 followed by 100 zeros.

1998 • Larry and Sergey leave Stanford and receive $100,000 from an investor to help set up their first headquarters in a friend's garage in California. Google launches to the world.

1999 • Larry and Sergey raise $25 million to help grow Google. Headquarters move to Palo Alto. Google Doodles are introduced. Yoshka, the first office dog, comes to work at Google.

2000 • Google launches AdWords, a revolutionary online advertising program.

2001 • Eric Schmidt becomes Google's CEO.

2004 • Google goes public. Google launches Gmail. Company headquarters move to Googleplex in Mountain View, California.

2005 • Google acquires Android. Google launches Google Earth and Google Maps.

2006 • Google acquires YouTube. Google becomes the number one search engine in the world. The word "google" is added to the dictionary.

2008 • Google launches Google Chrome, a web browser.

2010 • Self-driving car project begins.

2011 • Google Maps offers maps of building and airport interiors.

2012 • Google Drive launches.

2013 • Google is the most visited website in the world. Project Loon is launched.

2015 • Google starts testing self-driving cars. Larry and Sergey create Alphabet, a new parent company. Google is the largest company under the Alphabet umbrella.

2017 • Google becomes the most valuable brand in the world.

Are You a Future Noogler?

Here are examples of real questions asked by Larry, Sergey, and other Googlers during real Google interviews. How would you do?

Question 1:

10, 9, 60, 90, 70—what's the next number in the series?

Answer: 66. Why? Spell out each of the numbers—ten, nine, sixty, ninety, seventy. The first number (ten) is the largest number you can spell with three letters (bigger than one, two, and six). The second number (nine) is the biggest number you can spell with four letters. Sixty is the biggest number you can spell with five letters. Ninety is the biggest number you can spell with six letters. Seventy is the biggest number you can spell with seven letters. So . . . sixty-six is the biggest number you can spell with eight letters.

Question 2:

If you had a stack of pennies as tall as the Empire State Building, could you fit them all in one room?

Answer: The question is not asking you to come up with the exact number of pennies in this ridiculous situation but rather to answer yes or no to the question. Could all of these pennies fit into one room? You only need to estimate the number in order to answer the question, so let's think about it. The Empire State Building is 102 stories tall, but you probably don't know that. What you do know is that it's about a hundred times taller than a one-story house, which is also the height of one room. So all you need to ponder is whether a hundred stacks of pennies stretching from the floor to the ceiling could fit into a room. Sure! In fact, one hundred stacks of pennies would fit into any room—even the smallest one.

Questions 3:

What is the best way to find a needle in a haystack?

Answer: Two answers are often given by future Nooglers. One, you could bring a large and powerful magnet to the haystack and search for it manually. The only thing that will be attracted to the magnet is the needle. Two, you could burn down the haystack. After it cools, the needle should be the only thing left there.

Question 4:

How many times a day do all three hands of an analog watch (with an hour, minute, and second hand) overlap?

Answer: 22 times

a.m.—12:00, 1:05, 2:11, 3:16, 4:22, 5:27, 6:33, 7:38, 8:44, 9:49, 10:55

p.m.—12:00, 1:05, 2:11, 3:16, 4:22, 5:27, 6:33, 7:38, 8:44, 9:49, 10:55

Question 5:

Why are manholes round?

Answer: This is a classic interview question with several good answers, including that round covers are easiest to manufacture, roll, and line up with the opening. But the most important answer is that no part of a round cover could fall through a circular opening, as other shapes could fall through. That means the heavy manhole cover won't fall on any workers below or slip out of place for the pedestrians above.

Source Notes

Introduction

page

viii *"we see being great at something as a starting point"*: Google, "Tea Things."

Chapter 1—Larry Page

2 *"I decided to either become a professor"*: Schmidt, Rosenberg, and Eagle, *How Google Works*, Foreword.

4 *"I was really lucky"*: Vise, *The Google Story*, 24.

5 *"It was huge, and it cost a lot of money"*: Ibid., 24.

   "typing Frog and Toad Together *into his computer"*: Ibid., 24.

6 *Larry and Carl took apart all the family's power tools:* Ibid., 24.

8 *The key to success was to* combine *innovative technologies with a successful business strategy"*: D'Onfro, "Larry Page."

   Over time, Larry developed a passion for time, rhythm, and speed in music: Miguel Helft, "How Music Education Influenced Larry Page," Fortune.com, November 18, 2014.

Chapter 2—Sergey Brin

11 *"They see enormous mountains"*: Dan Fost, "Google

Co-founder Sergey Brin Wants More Computers in Schools," latimesblogs.latimes.com, October 28, 2009.

15   *"We started with nothing. We were poor":* Brandt, *The Google Guys,* 28.

     Mikhail and Yevgenia kept their sense of humor: Vise, *The Google Story,* 27.

16   *studying how weather conditions affect space travel:* Ibid., 25.

17   *he could solve graduate-level math problems:* Brandt, *The Google Guys,* 29.

19   *"Yes, advanced swimming":* Vise, *The Google Story,* 28.

21   *"I thought [Sergey] was pretty obnoxious. He had really strong opinions about things, and I guess I did, too":* Battelle, "The Birth of Google."

Chapter 3—Searching for an Idea

22   *"Anything you can imagine probably is doable":* Diamandis and Kotler, *Bold,* 136.

26   *"It turns out, people who win the Nobel Prize have citations from ten thousand different papers":* Vise, *The Google Story,* 37.

29   *"We started working really, really hard on it":* Ibid., 12.

30   *"We saw that a thousand results weren't necessarily as useful as ten good ones":* David Sheff, "Playboy Interview: Google Guys," *Playboy,* July 27, 2009, www.playboy.com/articles/playboy-interview-google-guys.

Chapter 4—In Search of the Future

34   *"You should try to do things most people would not":* McPherson, *Sergey Brin and Larry Page,* 62.

35 *"We would just borrow a few machines"*: Vise, *The Google Story*, 40.

38 *"Look, if this Google thing pans out, then great"*: Battelle, "The Birth of Google."

Chapter 5—Launching to the World

39 *"It's often easier to make progress when you're really ambitious"*: Diamandis and Kotler, *Bold*, 136.

"This is the single best idea I have heard in years. I want to be part of this": McPherson, *Sergey Brin and Larry Page*, 38.

Chapter 6—Let's Be the Good Guys

45 *"If you're not doing some things that are crazy, then you're doing the wrong things"*: Steven Levy, "Google's Larry Page on Why Moon Shots Matter," *Wired*, January 17, 2013, www.wired.com/2013/01/ff-qa-larry-page.

49 *"We should show people in the world that people at Google care about Halloween"*: Vise, *The Google Story*, 75.

"What about aliens? Let's put aliens on the homepage": Edwards, *I'm Feeling Lucky*, 122.

Chapter 7—In Search of Googleyness

53 *"We do go out of our way to recruit people who are a little different"*: Poundstone, *Are You Smart Enough*, 57.

That meant every Googler must work well with others and contribute something unique to Google: Schmidt, Rosenberg, and Eagle, *How Google Works*, 121.

55 *One day he served lobsters that were on sale because they only had one claw*: Edwards, *I'm Feeling Lucky*, 91.

56 *"Could you teach me something complicated I don't know?"*:
Schmidt, Rosenberg, and Eagle, *How Google Works*, 95.

"Would you be happy or sad about it?": Poundstone,
Are You Smart Enough, 46.

*Sergey conducted an interview while dressed in a full-size
cow costume:* Edwards, *I'm Feeling Lucky*, 9.

*Sergey conducted an interview while wearing Rollerblades
and athletic shorts:* Ibid., 9.

57 *"Here's your space over here. There are a bunch of parts over
there. Make your own computer"*: Ibid., 17.

58 *Some of Google's greatest products evolved from the 20
percent rule:* Schmidt, Rosenberg, and Eagle, *How Google
Works*, 227.

Chapter 8—Google's Search for Profitability

60 *"Always delivered more than expected"*: Renée Warren,
"101 Best Inspirational Quotes for Entrepreneurs,"
Business Insider, September 7, 2013, www.business
insider.com/101-best-inspirational-quotes-entrepre
neurs-2013-9.

61 *"What if ads weren't intrusive and annoying?"*: 2014
Google Annual Report, www.sec.gov/Archives/
edgar/data/1288776/000128877615000008/
goog2014123110-k.htm.

63 *Larry and Sergey didn't think anyone was good enough for
the job:* Vise, *The Google Story*, 107.

64 *"We argued for at least ninety minutes"*: Ibid., 106.

65 *it was the best argument he had had in a very long time:*
Ibid., 106.

Chapter 9—Thinking Outside the Search Box

66 *"Our job is to think of the thing you haven't thought of yet that you really need":* Miguel Helft, "Fortune Exclusive: Larry Page on Google," *Fortune,* December 11, 2012, www.fortune.com /2012/12/11/fortune-exclusive-larry-page-on-google.

71 *"We try things. Remember, we* celebrate *our failures":* Siegler, "Schmidt Talks Wave's Death."

"The only way you are going to have success is to have lots of failures first": Vise, *The Google Story,* 16.

Chapter 10—Googleplex

80 *"We want Google to be the third half of your brain":* Jay Yarow, "Sergey Brin: 'We Want Google to Be the Third Half of Your Brain'," BusinessInsider.com, September 8, 2010.

With over seven million square feet of office space: Connor Dougherty, "Google Plans New Headquarters and a City Fears Being Overrun," *New York Times,* February 25, 2015.

82 *In the Googleplex lobby, a live search board displays:* Poundstone, *Are You Smart Enough,* 3.

Chapter 11—Behind Door X

87 *"We should be building great things that don't exist":* Shara Tibken, "Google's Page: We Should Be Building Great Things That Don't Exist," Cnet, May 15, 2013. www.cnet .com/news/googles-page-we-should-be-building -great -things-that-dont-exist.

Chapter 12—A B C D E F GOOGLE

96 *"We won't stop asking 'What if?' and then working hard to find the answer":* Alphabet, 2004 Founders' IPO Letter,

www.abc.xyz/investor/founders-letters/2004/ipo-letter
.html.

97 *"Alphabet is mostly a collection of companies"*: Larry Page,
"G is for Google," Alphabet, August 10, 2015, www
.googleblog.blogspot.com/2015/08/google-alphabet.html.

98 *"Our model is to have a strong CEO who runs each business,
with Sergey and me in service to them as needed"*: Cade Metz,
"Alphabet Lets Google Chase Moonshots and Still Stay
Profitable," *Wired,* August 10, 2015, www.wired.com
/2015/08/alphabet-lets-google-chase-moonshots-stay
-profitable.

101 *"Everyone wants to be successful but I want to be looked back
on as being very innovative"*: Peter Jennings, "Persons of
the Week: Larry Page & Sergey Brin," ABC News,
February 20, 2004, www.abcnews.go.com/WNT/
PersonOfWeek/story?id=131833.

Are You a Future Noogler?

104 *Question 1:* Poundstone, *Are You Smart Enough*, 8.

105 *Question 2:* Poundstone, Ibid., 193.

Question 3: Brian Milligan "How to answer those bizarre
job interview questions" *BBC News,* June 13, 2013, www
.bbc.com/news/business-22844117.

106 *Question 4:* Poundstone, *Are You Smart Enough*, 193.

Question 5: Erin McCarthy, "Why Are Manhole Covers
Round?" *Mental Floss,* January 7, 2015, www.mentalfloss
.com/article/60929/why-are-manhole-covers-round.

Bibliography

Alphabet. "A New Way Forward for Mobility." www.google
   .com/selfdrivingcar.

Balise, Julie. "Office Space: Google's Campus Feels as Big as
   the Internet Itself." *San Francisco Chronicle,* January 5,
   2015. www.sfgate.com/business/article/Office-Space
   -Google-s-campus-feels-as-big-as-5992389.php.

Battelle, John. "The Birth of Google." *Wired,* August 1, 2005.
   www.wired.com/2005/08/battelle.

Brandt, Richard L. *The Google Guys.* New York: Penguin
   Group, 2011.

D'Onfro, Jillian. "The Spectacular Life of Google Founder
   and Alphabet CEO Larry Page." *Business Insider,* March
   17, 2016. www.businessinsider.com/the-life-career-of-larry
   -page-2016-3.

Diamandis, Peter H., and Steven Kotler. *Bold: How to Go Big,
   Create Wealth and Impact the World.* New York: Simon and
   Schuster, 2015.

Edwards, Douglas. *I'm Feeling Lucky: The Confessions of
   Google Employee Number 59.* New York: Houghton Mifflin
   Harcourt, 2011.

Google. "From the Garage to Googleplex." www.google.com /intl/en/about/our-story.

Google. Google Founders' Letter, 2013. www.abc.xyz/investor /founders-letters/2013.

Google. Google Self-Driving Car Project Monthly Report, October 2016. https://static.googleusercontent.com/ media/www.google.com/en//selfdrivingcar/files/reports/ report-1016.pdf.

Google. "Ten Things We Know to Be True." www.google.com /intl/en/about/philosophy.

He, Laura. "Google's Secrets of Innovation: Empowering Its Employees." *Forbes,* March 29, 2013. www.forbes.com /sites/laurahe/2013/03/29/googles-secrets-of-innovation -empowering-its-employees/#56c7974e57e7.

Kelion, Leo. "Google Tests Balloons to Beam Internet from Near Space." *BBC News,* June 15, 2013.

McPherson, Stephanie Sammartino. *Sergey Brin and Larry Page: Founders of Google.* Minneapolis: Twenty-First Century Books, 2011.

North, John. *The 5 Stages to Entrepreneurial Success.* Evolve Global Publishing, 2017.

Poundstone, William. *Are You Smart Enough to Work at Google?* New York: Back Bay Book/Little, Brown, 2012.

"Project Loon." www.x.company/loon.

Schmidt, Eric, Jonathan Rosenberg, and Alan Eagle. *How Google Works.* New York: Grand Central Publishing, 2014.

Scott, Virginia. *Google: Corporations That Changed the World*. Westport, CT: Greenwood Press, 2008.

Siegler, M. G. "Schmidt Talks Wave's Death: 'We Celebrate Our Failures.'" Techcrunch.com, August 4, 2010. www .techcrunch.com/2010/08/04/google-wave-eric-schmidt.

Vise, David A., and Mark Malseed. *The Google Story*. New York: Bantam Dell, 2005.

Wohlsen, Marcus. "Why Google Must Now Also Rule the Physical World." *Wired*, May 21, 2014. www.wired .com/2014/05/why-google-needs-to-master-the -physical-world-even-more-than-the-internet.

Wojcicki, Susan. "The Eight Pillars of Innovation." Google: Think with Google, July 2011. www.thinkwithgoogle .com/marketing-resources/8-pillars-of-innovation.

Lowey Bundy Sichol is the author
of *From an Idea to . . .* , the world's first business
biographies for kids. Lowey is also the founder of
Case Marketing, a specialized writing firm that
researches and composes case studies for business
schools and corporations. Her case studies have
been read by MBA students all over the world.
Lowey received a BA from Hamilton College and
an MBA from the Tuck School of Business at
Dartmouth. Lowey lives in Illinois with her hus-
band, Adam, three children, and two dogs who,
unlike Yoshka, like to jump on the FedEx and
UPS delivery people and tear open their packages.
Look for Lowey online at loweybundysichol.com.

Like Larry and Sergey, Lowey also has a father who loves computers. In 1981, he brought home the original IBM PC. However, instead of learning computer programming like Larry and Sergey, Lowey and her brothers played games on it by pounding on the keyboard as hard as they could. (This made her dad really mad!)

Lowey wrote her first email from a crowded computer room at the University of Edinburgh in Scotland in 1995, while she was studying abroad. She had to read a ten-page manual to figure out how to do it!

FROM AN IDEA TO

DISNEY

How Imagination Built
a World of Magic

by **LOWEY BUNDY SICHOL**

illustrated by **C. S. JENNINGS**

FROM AN IDEA TO

NIKE

How Marketing Made
Nike a Global Success

by **LOWEY BUNDY SICHOL**

illustrated by **C. S. JENNINGS**

FROM AN IDEA TO
LEGO
The Building Bricks Behind the World's Largest Toy Company
by LOWEY BUNDY SICHOL
illustrated by C. S. JENNINGS